THE TIME IS NOW, THE PERSON IS YOU    BY NIDO QUBEIN

# This Book Belongs To:

# THE TIME IS NOW, THE PERSON IS YOU

A treasury
of quotes & thoughts
to motivate you at work
and inspire you in life

NIDO R. QUBEIN

© 1997 All rights reserved by Nido R. Qubein

Library of Congress Cataloging in Publication Data

ISBN 0-939975-12-2

For quantity purchases of this book contact:

Executive Press
806 Westchester Drive
P. O. Box 6008
High Point, NC  27262  USA
(336)889-3010, Facsimile (336)885-3001
www.nidoqubein.com

Printed in the United States of America

To My Children:

Ramsey, Deena, Cristina, Michael.

May this small book make

a big difference in your life.

Love,
Dad

# ALSO BY NIDO R. QUBEIN

ACHIEVING PEAK PERFORMANCE

COMMUNICATE LIKE A PRO

HOW TO GET ANYTHING YOU WANT

HOW TO BE A GREAT COMMUNICATOR

HOW TO BE A GREAT SALES PROFESSIONAL

STAIRWAY TO SUCCESS

MARKETING PROFESSIONAL SERVICES

HOW TO POSITION YOURSELF FOR SUCCESS

HOW TO SELL, SERVE AND SUCCEED

THE CRESTCOM MANAGEMENT SERIES

# Thank you

To all those who nurtured my soul, nourished my heart, and cheered me on along the journey of life, I offer my deepest gratitude. You're my family and my friends; my business associates and speaker colleagues; my scholarship foundation partners and community leaders. You're awesome .

You showed me the power of love and the impact of courage. You instilled in me the importance of principles and the clarity of values. You explained to me the difference between risk avoidance and risk management. You taught me the joy of giving and the virtue of sacrifice. And, most importantly, you focused me on significance not success. What heroes, models and mentors you've been!

I love you,

Nido Qubein

# About this book

This is a short, topical collection of quotations selected from various books, video programs, audio cassettes, and magazine columns Nido Qubein has authored over the years.

Nido's speeches, writing, television programs, and consultations have reached millions of people from border to border, coast to coast, and over thirty countries across the globe.

May the power of these ideas influence your life, your family and your business. Indeed, the time is now to pursue your dreams. And the person is you.

# Contents

Wherever you are,
whatever your circumstances
may be, whatever misfortune
you may have suffered,
the music of your life has not gone.
It's inside you —
if you listen to it, you can play it.

# Achievement

Winners compare their achievements with their goals, while losers compare their achievements with those of other people.

Your present circumstances don't determine where you can go; they merely determine where you start.

Achieving your vision doesn't mean you've reached the end of the line. It simply means that you've come to a new starting place.

Make a strong and permanent commitment to invest your talents only in pursuits that deserve your best efforts.

Being genuinely helpful
to other people not only makes
you feel better about yourself...
it is good business.

# ANXIETY

Conquer the anxiety habit, and you can reduce your chances of distress.  Don't worry about it — do it!

People worry for only two reasons.  Either they stand to lose something they want to keep, or they stand not to gain something they want to get.  If keeping something you have costs you your peace of mind, or if something you stand to gain takes you to the brink of distress, it makes sense to ask yourself whether what you are worried over is worth the price.

95% of what we worry about never happens!

Anxiety is the currency of the insecure.

*19*

Success is finding and doing
to the best of your ability,
in each moment of your life,
what you enjoy most doing,
what you can do best,
and what has the greatest possibility
of providing the means to live
as you would like to live
in relation to yourself
and all persons you value.

# ATTITUDE

You can't think your way into acting positively, but you can act your way into thinking positively.

Nobody likes to be around a person who is always looking at the dark side of life.

Whether you are a success or failure in life has little to do with your circumstances; it has much more to do with your choices!

Simmering resentment saps energy.

Hatred is the most destructive force on earth.  It does the most damage to those who harbor it.

What if you could be
anything, or anybody,
you chose to be?
Think about it!
What would you
choose to be?

# CHANGE

Change brings opportunity.

The organization that can't communicate can't change, and the corporation that can't change is dead.

Are you a thermometer or a thermostat? A thermometer only reflects the temperature of its environment, adjusting to the situation. But a thermostat initiates action to change the temperature in its environment.

For many people, change is more threatening than challenging. They see it as the destroyer of what is familiar and comfortable rather than the creator of what is new and exciting.

When a goal matters
enough to a person, that person
will find a way to accomplish
what at first seemed impossible.

# COMMITMENT

If what you are doing is worth doing, hang in there until it is done.

A decision is made with the brain. A commitment is made with the heart. Therefore, a commitment is much deeper and more binding than a decision.

If what you're working for really matters, you'll give it all you've got.

Make a strong commitment to reach your full potential as a human being.

A commitment is like your signature on a contract: it binds you to a course of action.

The power comes from within you. It's there and you may not even know it.

The word success
does not contain an "i."
The first vowel is "u,"
and until we learn to think you
instead of I, our batting average
in communication
and in human relations
will be close to zero.

# COMMUNICATION

The genius who can't communicate is intellectually impotent.

High-powered communicators learn to focus words the way a laser beam focuses light.

Courtesy is the oil that lubricates the machinery of communication.

Say what you mean, precisely what you mean, and only what you mean.

Don't interrupt, but be interruptible.

A "monologue in duet" happens when I think up what I'm going to say while you're saying what you thought up while I was talking.

You can live every day of your life.
You can be alive
to the tips of your fingers.
You can accomplish virtually
any worthwhile goal
you set for yourself.

# EDUCATION

With life-long education, learning becomes a renewable resource.

Training teaches people to follow prescriptions. Education teaches people to make choices.

Make education a continuing, never-ending process.

Training is anchored to the past.  Education looks toward the future.

Teaching people skills without giving them a vision for a better future — a vision based on common values — is only training.

Training teaches how.  Education teaches why.

Losers do what
is required of them,
or even less;
but winners always
do more than is required —
and they do it
with enthusiasm.

# ENTHUSIASM

Enthusiasm is the color of inspiration and courage.

Enthusiasm is the light of creativity and insight.

Enthusiasm is a positive inner force that makes things happen, a gracious and polite bid for attention, a method of diplomacy and persuasion, a cooperative spirit, an excitement for life.

Greet every person you meet cheerfully and enthusiastically. Nobody can fake cheerfulness and enthusiasm very long. You'll either quit trying or improve your outlook.

Enthusiastic people experience life from the inside out.

*31*

Each of us
has the freedom to choose
how we will respond
to the circumstances
in which we find
ourselves.

# FAITH

Those who base their lives on the belief that a loving God is acting in their behalf tend to see problems as opportunities for growth.

———

Material success may result in the accumulation of possessions; but only spiritual success will enable you to enjoy them.

———

Spiritual values transcend the material artifacts that we can touch and see.  They take us into the realm of beauty, inspiration and love.

———

If you believe you can, and believe it strongly enough, you will be amazed at what you can do.

No mistake
you could ever make
would strip you of your value
as a human being.
Most mistakes detour
you only slightly on your road
to fulfilling your purpose.

# FUTURE

The past can be a wonderful place to visit, but you wouldn't want to live there.

———

Many people are unable to prepare for the future because they're too busy rehearsing the past.

———

The past is over.  Enjoy the good memories, use the bad ones as lessons in life, and get ready to make some new ones.  Your focus should be on the future.

———

Creative people look at the future as a big adventure instead of a looming threat.

———

May the future you create exceed your fondest expectations!

When we carve out a niche
for ourselves
in our imagined future,
and decide that we won't be happy
until we achieve it,
we can only feel
threatened and anxious
over anything
that stands in our way.

# GIVING

Those who sow abundantly reap abundantly.

You cannot enrich the soul of another, without being enriched yourself.

The key to your success is to be sensitive enough to understand what other people want, and generous enough to help them get it.

Many people looking for meaning in their lives find it by losing themselves in causes greater than they are.

You cannot give what you do not possess.

The surest route to success today is to find out what others want, and look for ways to provide it.

Learn to be kind to yourself.
Keep a list of your triumphs
and successes.
As you focus on what you
have done, you will have
more confidence
in what you can do.

# GOALS

Goal-setting illuminates the road to success just
as runway lights illuminate the landing field for an
incoming aircraft.

Only when your memories are more important to you
than your goals are you old.

Whatever keeps you from reaching your goal for today
had better be important — it's costing you a day
of your life!

Goals are simply a way of breaking a vision into
smaller, workable units.

Goals help you keep in perspective what's really
important so you don't spend all of your time doing
what seems urgent.

Self-confidence is often
little more than a feeling,
way down in the pit
of your stomach,
that you can do
something that reason
says is impossible.

# HAPPINESS

People who are looking for something to make them happy, somehow never seem to find it.  Yet those who find a way to be happy while they are looking for something, typically find what they are looking for.

Success is an empty attainment if it doesn't bring happiness.

Accept each moment as a gift to be received with joy.

Those who spend their lives searching for happiness never find it, while those who search for meaning, purpose, and strong personal relationships find that happiness usually comes to them as a by-product of those three things.

The good moments of the present are the good memories you will carry into your future.

Learn to accept
constructive criticism
and to ignore petty
criticism.

# HUMOR

The person who can laugh often, and who finds humor in even the most stressful events, can keep going when others are falling beside the way.

---

Learn to look for the humor in every situation — you'll live longer and have a lot more fun.

---

Cultivate a sense of humor. Humor is the pleasant lubricant of life.

---

Nothing softens the blows of life like a good sense of humor.

---

When you can see the humor in embarrassing situations, they cease to be stressful.

---

Develop the ability to laugh at yourself.

Putting things off has seldom
been associated with winning.
It's the losers who
wait for things to happen.
The winners in the game of life
make things happen.

# KNOWLEDGE

Knowledge is to creativity what a bed of coals is to a fire. It provides a reservoir of resources to keep the creative fires burning. So to develop creativity, acquire a thirst for knowledge.

If learning were easy, our mental power would never be developed.

Competence leads to confidence.

It's our enemies from whom we learn the most.

In an age in which most things that glitter are plastic, seek to find some nuggets of gold.  Treasure them.

Acquire a learning mentality.

Admire your heroes. Adapt from your models. Learn from your mentors.

*45*

People
who are not challenged
will not exert themselves
to succeed.

# LEADERSHIP

Behavior that goes consistently unrewarded will eventually be discontinued.

People don't respond to what you say; they respond to what they understand you to say.

Good leaders must become what they want their followers to become.

High morale can't flourish in a workplace full of conflict.

The leader who can't communicate can't create the conditions that motivate.

To be a great person, walk hand-in-hand and side-by-side with great people.

*47*

Professionals are willing
to take intelligent risks,
accepting the possibility
of failure
as a fair price
for the opportunity
to grow.

# LIFE

Accumulate good memories.

If you could view your life as you do a highway from an airliner, many of the detours and curves would make more sense.

Remember that the cards you're dealt are less important than the way you play your hand.

There's so much to see, to do, to be!  Life is full of choices.

The situations you encounter in life generally fall into three categories: Those you want to influence, those you'd like to influence, and those that are not worth influencing.

Losers blame their circumstances; winners rise above their circumstances.

*49*

The person who finishes
another's sentences,
denies another's right to a
differing opinion,
and approaches others
with suspicion is destined
to spend a great deal
of time alone.

# LISTENING

Self-centered people tend to monopolize the talking; secure people tend to monopolize the listening.

Talking when nobody is listening is as futile as trying to cut paper with half a pair of scissors.

Listen at least twice as much as you talk — others will hear twice as much of what you say.

People who are poor listeners will find few who are willing to come to them with useful information.

Forget your ability to think faster than another person talks — everybody has it, but only the foolish use it.

*51*

Many people deny themselves
the pleasure of living life
to the fullest because
they follow limited visions.
They dream modest dreams,
so they compile
modest achievements.
The limiting factor
is not their capacity
to achieve but their willingness
to believe in themselves.

# LOVE

Only when you love and are loved can you reach your full potential as a human being.

If you practice the principle of love, you will soon find your feelings taking their cue from your actions.

Love is the most positive force on earth, and each of us can cultivate it.

Learn to be gracious — whether you win or lose.

Human beings have both an overwhelming capacity to love and an overriding need to love and be loved.

Cultivate love by banishing hatred.

Some people procrastinate
so much that all they can do
is run around
like firefighters all day —
putting out fires
that should not have
gotten started
in the first place.

# PERSONAL DEVELOPMENT

No one ever becomes perfect; but anyone can improve.

A habit is nothing but an action that has become automatic.

Your most frequently used tool should be your imagination, not your memory.

Don't mistake the difficult for the impossible.

Disguising incompetence doesn't alter the basic condition.

If you would be successful, first you must walk hand-in-hand and side-by-side with successful people.

When you find yourself on a plateau, look for another level.

The trouble with many plans
is that they are based on the way
things are now.  To be successful,
your personal plan must focus
on what you want,
not what you have.

# PERSONAL EXCELLENCE

Focus on fixing the problem, not the blame.

An extraordinary person is someone who consistently does the things ordinary people can't do or won't do.

The difference between mediocrity and excellence lies in inner qualities and not external skills.

It is important to measure your performance against your past success, but it is even more important to measure your performance against your potential.

Losers ask "Can I do it?"  Winners ask "How can I do it?" Losers are guided by what's impossible. Winners are guided by what's possible.

To acquire balance means
to achieve that happy medium
between the minimum
and the maximum
that represents your optimum.
The minimum is the least
you can get by with.
The maximum is the most
you're capable of.
The optimum is the amount
or degree of anything
that is most favorable toward
the ends you desire.

# PERSPECTIVE

Up close, the earth looks flat.  From outer space, it's round.  The difference is in perspective.

---

Seek to know others — you'll be amazed at how it will help you understand yourself.

---

When something becomes personal, it becomes important.

---

We're inclined to excuse in ourselves behavior that we find unacceptable in others.

---

When we see things in perspective, we see them in their proper relationships as to value or importance.

---

What you are and hope to be is the way you experience yourself; but other people experience you by what you do.

*59*

When we dread doing
something, it's usually easier—
for the moment—
to come up with an excuse.
Unfortunately,
most of us find the dread
to be counterproductive
because the longer we dread
the task,
the worse it seems.

# PROCRASTINATION

The interesting thing about procrastination is that it has more to do with what we fail to do than with what we do.

---

Procrastination is a thief which robs you of money by stealing your time.

---

Procrastination is delaying anything you need or want to do, until later — when there is no valid reason to do so.

---

The way most of us procrastinate is to do nothing about anything we should be doing something about.

---

If you put everything off until you're sure of it, you'll never get anything done.

You won't know
whether you're moving
toward your goals
unless you have some way
of measuring the motion.

—————————

# PURPOSE

To live, you must have a purpose to guide you.

—————

Set goals that are consistent with your purpose in life.

—————

Above all, be true to yourself, and as surely as day follows night, you can't be false to anyone.

—————

In choosing your purpose in life, you have to answer three big questions:  Who am I?  What am I doing here? Where am I going?

—————

Do your tasks. Achieve your goals. Live with your purpose.

People can be unreliable
and disloyal;
possessions can lose their value;
jobs that once stimulated you
can become boring.
But principles remain steady
through it all.

# RELATIONSHIPS

Fixing the blame is never important, and fixing the relationship is never unimportant.

———

Grudges are like tumors; they can live and grow only when they're eating on you.

———

People who put career first may end up with gold-plated resumes and rusted-out family lives.

———

People who invariably put themselves first will find that others tend to put them last.

———

When you like yourself, you will gravitate toward people who like you.

———

Your acquaintances fall into three basic categories: Those who will be cheering for you whether you win or lose; those who will be pulling for you to fail; those who don't care one way or the other. Choose well!

*65*

When you identify something
that you do well,
that you enjoy doing,
and that supports the values
that are important to you,
you have defined success
in your terms.

# RISK

The only way to keep from making mistakes is to do nothing — and that's the biggest mistake of all.

The process of growing and learning always involves risk.

People stay in ruts because it takes less effort to follow the rut than to get out of it.

Unconscious choices put you at the mercy of the dice roll.

Successful people don't avoid risks. They learn to manage them. They don't dive off cliffs into unexplored waters. They learn how deep the water is, and make sure there are no hidden obstacles. Then they plunge in.

Most of us tend to suffer
from "agenda anxiety,"
the feeling that what we want
to say to others
is more important
than what we think
they might
want to say to us.

# SALES

If you create tension, you get resistance!  If you create trust, you get response!

---

People buy from salespeople they trust.

---

In the marketplace of life, the seller may set the price; but it is always the buyer who determines the value.

---

Objections are to the salesperson what symptoms are to the medical doctor;  they point to a problem that must be dealt with.

---

The ultimate test of your selling effectiveness is your power to persuade plenty of prospects to purchase your product at a profit.

---

Objections are the salesperson's most valuable source of feedback.

Total, unconditional
acceptance of yourself
is the first step in building
a positive
self-image.

# SELF-ESTEEM

A strong awareness that you are loved by God provides the most solid foundation for building high self-esteem.

People who think only of themselves, and what they want, find it hard to be happy with anything they get.

Make it a habit to say nice things about yourself, to yourself. You'll find that you like yourself better.

Integrity breeds high self-esteem — and it earns you a lot of friends as well.

What other people think about you is your reputation. What you think about yourself represents your true worth.

When you accept yourself totally, you are free to accept other people.

If you believe you can,
and believe it strongly enough,
you'll be amazed at what
you can do.

# SPEECH

No speaker is so good that practice won't improve the presentation.  Practice gives confidence to the speaker and polish to the speech.

Most people tend to remember more about the feeling a speech creates than they do about the content of the message it delivers.

What you say does not have nearly the impact of the way you say it.

Brevity is the very heart of a good speech.

A good story is to a speech what a window is to a house — it lets in the light.

If you would be successful,
first you must walk hand-in-hand
and side-by-side with
successful people.

# SUCCESS

Success doesn't come to you; you must go to it.  The trail is well-traveled and well marked.  If you want to walk it, you can.

Success rarely comes to those who are expecting failure.

Success is not a matter of luck, an accident of birth, or a reward for virtue.

Success comes to most truly successful people as a series of little successes, rather than as one big break.

Success is not an either/or proposition: either work or pleasure; either the party or the grindstone.  Success consists of finding a happy balance between work and pleasure.  In fact, truly successful people make their work a part of their pleasure.

Successful,
self-starting individuals
seek responsibility.
They take calculated risks,
they don't make excuses
to cover up their
inactivity.

# TIME

Do you manage your time, or does your time manage you?

If a task is worth doing, it is worth doing at the earliest reasonable time.  If it is not worth doing, forget it!

You're wasting your time when you try to answer questions people are not asking.

The key to scheduling your time is to focus on objectives, not on activities.

The time is now, the person is you.

Nothing gets accomplished "sooner or later."  It gets accomplished at a specific time and specific place.

The key to emotional health
is to learn how to handle grief.
The person who reacts
to sorrow only with anger
becomes embittered,
hardened,
and cynical.

# VALUES

What you value determines the principles by which you measure your behavior.

Applying your talents without reference to your values and principles is like using your car's accelerator without touching the steering wheel.

When we perceive the way things are as the way things ought to be, our lives are in harmony.

What matters is not so much how you got to be the way you are now, but what you do with the person you have become.

When your life is possession-centered, the important thing is what you have; when it is principle-centered, the important thing is who and what you are.

Many potential innovators
failed to dream,
and many dreamers
failed to make their dreams
become reality.

# WORK

If you work only on days you feel like working, you'll never amount to much.

———

Most of us miss our best opportunities in life because they come to us disguised as hard work.

———

Your best bet for a good job is to do the best you can with the one you have right now.

———

Motivation without mobilization causes frustration.

———

You may have the loftiest goals, the highest ideals, the noblest dreams; but remember this, nothing works unless you do.

———

If you do your best only when you feel like doing your best, your work will probably be pretty shabby.

# ABOUT THE AUTHOR

Nido Qubein is chairman of four companies: Creative Services, Inc. (an international management consulting firm), Great Harvest Bread Co. (250 stores in 40 states and Canada), Business Life, Inc. (publisher of bizlife Magazine), and McNeill Lehman, Inc. (a national public relations agency).

He is a partner in several other companies and serves on the boards of 17 universities, corporations, and community organizations, including BB&T Corporation, High Point University, Economic Development Corporation, Mount Olive College, and Bryan School of Business. He is the founder of the National Speakers Association Foundation in Phoenix.

He has been the recipient of many honors, including a Doctor of Laws degree, the Ellis Island Medal of Honor, The Cavett (known as the Oscar of the speaking profession), Toastmasters International Golden Gavel, the Sales and Marketing International Hall of Fame, and Citizen of the Year in High Point, North Carolina, where he resides.

He speaks each year to more than a hundred audiences at conventions, sales meetings, and executive conferences. He has written many books and recorded scores of audio and video programs, which have been translated into several languages.

For information on Nido Qubein's speeches, books,
cassettes and consulting call or write:

Creative Services, Inc.
806 Westchester Drive
P. O. Box 6008
High Point, NC  27262  USA
Telephone (336)889-3010
Facsimile (336)885-3001
www.nidoqubein.com